wraps

wraps

Jennie Shapter

photography by William Lingwood

RYLAND
PETERS
& SMALL

LONDON NEW YORK

First published in the
United States in 2007
by Ryland Peters & Small
519 Broadway, 5th Floor
New York, NY 10012
www.rylandpeters.com

10 9 8 7 6 5 4 3 2 1

ISBN-10: 1-84597-383-6
ISBN-13: 978-1-84597-383-4

Library of Congress Cataloging-in-
Publication Data
Shapter, Jennie.
  Wraps / Jennie Shapter ; photography by
William Lingwood. -- 1st U.S. ed.
    p. cm.
  Includes index.
  ISBN-13: 978-1-84597-383-4
  1. Stuffed foods (Cookery) I. Title.
  TX836.S53 2007
  641.8'4--dc22

                          2006027798

Senior Designer Toni Kay
Commissioning Editor Julia Charles
Senior Editors
Clare Double, Lesley Malkin
Production Gemma Moules
Art Director Anne-Marie Bulat
Publishing Director Alison Starling

Food Stylist Jennie Shapter
Prop Stylist Liz Belton

Notes
• All spoon measurements are level
unless otherwise specified.
• All eggs are medium unless
otherwise specified. Uncooked or
partly cooked eggs should not be
served to the very young, the very
old, those with compromised immune
systems, or to pregnant women.

contents

introduction

Wraps and rolls with tantalizing fillings hidden within are ideal for almost any occasion. Perfect for summertime eating, this collection of recipes includes classic flavors with a modern twist and innovative contemporary combinations inspired by flavors from Europe, the American Southwest and Mexico, and the Middle and Far East. Whether you are looking for an appetizer or snack, a selection of light bites for a relaxed gathering, or an easy-to-prepare lunch or dinner dish, there is a recipe here to suit.

Tortillas make a great light alternative to bread, lending themselves to almost any hot or cold filling. They can be rolled and easily transported for picnics and packed lunches and are a great choice for informal eating, where everyone can fill their own. Tortillas are the obvious choice for a wrap but this selection also includes stylish vegetable wraps, using peppers, eggplant, and zucchini; French-style savory crêpes; Asian rice-paper and wonton wraps; and Japanese nori for sushi wraps.

Although you can buy ready-prepared wraps, making your own allows you to use the freshest of ingredients, indulge your favorite tastes, and control your calorie and fat intake. Tortilla wraps and chapattis are readily available in the supermarkets but I have included recipes for different sizes if you wish to make your own. Do experiment with herbs and spices to add flavor— there is nothing better than freshly made wraps filled while still warm from the pan! Just make sure you match the size of the wrap in the recipe to the size you make or purchase, or adjust the filling ingredients accordingly.

Asian wraps for spring rolls, wonton wraps, and Chinese pancakes are readily available from specialist stores and can be frozen. Crêpes are quick and easy to prepare and can be made in advance.

light bites

Buckwheat, with its distinctive earthy flavor, is the essential ingredient for blinis—the celebrated Russian pancakes traditionally served with caviar. These wraps are a variation on blinis, filled with smoked salmon, scrambled eggs, and asparagus. You could also add a little caviar or lumpfish roe, if wished.

buckwheat pancake wraps

2 oz. asparagus tips

4 eggs

¼ cup milk

1 tablespoon butter

2½ oz. smoked salmon, cut into strips

2 tablespoons chopped fresh dill

8 x 6-inch Buckwheat Pancakes, warmed (see page 63)

salt and freshly ground black pepper

fresh dill sprigs, to garnish

makes 8 serves 4

Blanch the asparagus in lightly salted water for 2 minutes. Drain, then refresh under cold water and pat dry. Cut the asparagus into 1-inch lengths.

Beat the eggs together with the milk and season with a little salt and plenty of black pepper. Melt the butter in a nonstick pan, add the egg mixture, and cook over a gentle heat, stirring until just starting to set. Stir in the asparagus and cook until the eggs are just scrambled. Fold in the smoked salmon and dill.

Fold the pancakes into quarters and fill with the scrambled egg mix. Put two pancakes on each serving plate, garnish with sprigs of dill, and serve immediately.

Halloumi is a Greek cheese that is fairly bland so lends itself to marinating with Mediterranean herbs before wrapping with pieces of grilled pepper. It is important to serve these hot while the cheese is soft as it becomes rubbery once cold.

2 tablespoons olive oil

grated zest and freshly squeezed juice of 1 lemon

1 teaspoon balsamic vinegar

2 teaspoons fresh thyme, chopped

8 oz. halloumi cheese or queso fresco, cut into 12 slices

1 large yellow bell pepper

2 large red bell peppers

freshly ground black pepper

salsa verde

3 tablespoons olive oil

1 garlic clove, finely chopped

2 inches cucumber, seeded and finely chopped

grated zest and freshly squeezed juice of 1 lime

2 tablespoons chopped fresh flat leaf parsley

2 tablespoons chopped fresh basil

1 teaspoon capers, rinsed and chopped

1 fresh green chile, finely chopped (optional)

makes 12 serves 4

halloumi and pepper wraps with salsa verde

Preheat the broiler to medium.

Mix the olive oil, lemon zest and juice, balsamic vinegar, thyme, and black pepper together in a shallow dish. Add the slices of cheese and set aside to marinate while preparing the peppers.

Halve the peppers lengthways and place on the broiler rack, skin-side up. Cook until they begin to soften and char. Do not overcook as they will be cooked again. Place in a large bowl, cover, and leave for 15 minutes. Meanwhile, mix the salsa verde ingredients, adding the chile if wished, and set aside to infuse.

Peel the skins off the peppers and remove the stalks and cores. Cut in half lengthways. Put a slice of cheese in the center of each pepper strip, allowing the cheese to protrude slightly over the edges of the pepper. Wrap the pepper over the cheese and secure with a toothpick. Put on a shallow baking sheet and brush with the remaining marinade.

Cook under a preheated medium-high broiler for 4–5 minutes on each side, or until the cheese softens and starts to brown and the peppers start to char. Serve three pepper wraps per person, drizzled with a little salsa verde.

Chapattis are unleavened breads typically served as an accompaniment to spicy dishes in northern India, so they make the perfect wraps for this spicy Indian chicken topped with yogurt and cucumber relish.

8 oz. skinless chicken breast fillets

2 tablespoons tandoori or tikka masala curry paste

3 tablespoons plain yogurt

2 teaspoons sunflower oil

4 x 6½-inch Chapattis (see page 62)

2 handfuls baby spinach leaves

minted cucumber relish

⅔ cup plain yogurt

¼ cucumber, seeded and diced

3 scallions, chopped

2 tablespoons chopped fresh mint

½ teaspoon ground cumin

freshly ground black pepper

makes 8 serves 4

Indian chicken wraps with minted cucumber relish

Preheat the oven to 400°F.

Cut the chicken fillets into strips. In a shallow dish, mix the curry paste, yogurt, and oil together. Add the chicken and toss to coat. Cover and leave to marinate for 30 minutes, or up to 4 hours, if time allows.

To make the relish, put the yogurt into a bowl with the cucumber, scallions, mint, and cumin. Mix together and season with black pepper. Chill.

Transfer the chicken pieces to a nonstick baking tray and bake for 15 minutes, or until the chicken juices run clear. Meanwhile, wrap the chapattis in foil and place in the oven to warm for the last 5 minutes, while the chicken is cooking.

Cut the chapattis in half. Top each half with a few strips of chicken and some spinach leaves, roll up, and secure with a toothpick. Serve 2 per person, along with a spoonful of the minted cucumber relish.

Spring rolls are best served immediately after cooking, but to keep last-minute preparation minimal make the filling up to 24 hours ahead. Fill the spring roll wrappers about an hour before cooking, but keep them covered so they remain moist until cooked.

mini spring rolls with chile dipping sauce

2 tablespoons sunflower oil

2 medium carrots, peeled and cut into matchsticks

½ cup snow peas, cut into matchsticks

¾ cup shiitake mushrooms, chopped

1 inch fresh ginger, peeled and grated

1 small fresh red chile, seeded and chopped

1 cup bean sprouts

2 scallions, thinly sliced

1 tablespoon light soy sauce

2 teaspoons all-purpose flour

8 x 8-inch square spring-roll wrappers

oil for deep-frying

a deep-fat fryer

chile dipping sauce

5 tablespoons sweet chile sauce

1 tablespoon light soy sauce

makes 16 serves 4

Heat the sunflower oil in a wok or frying pan and stir-fry the carrots, snow peas, mushrooms, and ginger for 1 minute. Add the chopped chile, bean sprouts, and scallions, and stir-fry for 1–2 minutes, or until the vegetables are tender-crisp. Remove from the heat, stir in the soy sauce, and set aside to cool.

Next, make the chile dipping sauce. Mix together the sweet chile sauce and soy sauce in a small bowl and transfer to a serving dish.

In a small bowl, mix the flour with 1 tablespoon water to make a paste. Cut the spring-roll wrappers in half diagonally and place under a damp cloth to keep moist. Remove one at a time to fill.

Divide the filling into four and put a quarter of one batch on the long cut side of a wrapper, placing it along the center, slightly in from the edge. Fold over the side flaps. Brush a little flour paste on the pointed end of the wrapper and roll up towards the point, pressing the end to seal. Repeat with the remaining wrappers. Keep covered until ready to cook.

Fill a deep-fryer with oil to the manufacturer's recommended level. Heat the oil to 350°F and deep-fry the rolls in batches for 2–3 minutes, until crisp and golden. Drain on paper towels. Serve hot with the chile dipping sauce.

3 lemongrass stalks

7 oz. ground lamb

2 shallots, finely chopped

2 teaspoons chopped fresh parsley

2 teaspoons chopped fresh cilantro

½ teaspoon ground allspice

1 small fresh red chile, seeded and finely chopped

flour, for dusting

2 tablespoons sunflower oil

½ small red bell pepper, seeded and cut into thin strips

12 white mini pita, warmed

12 crisp baby lettuce leaves

12 small sprigs fresh cilantro

minted cream

½ cup crème fraîche or sour cream

2 tablespoons fresh mint, chopped

salt and freshly ground black pepper

makes 12 serves 4

These fragrant mini-kebabs are popular in Morocco and Tunisia. The lemongrass skewers add a fragrance and opulence to the koftas, but you can use pre-soaked short wooden skewers if preferred.

lamb kofta wraps with minted cream

Slice the lemongrass in half widthways, then lengthways to make 12 sticks. In a bowl, mix the ground lamb, shallots, parsley, cilantro, allspice, and chile together. Divide into twelve and with lightly floured hands shape into 2-inch long finger shapes. Thread the koftas onto the lemongrass skewers.

In a small bowl mix the crème fraîche or sour cream and mint together and season with salt and freshly ground black pepper.

Heat the oil in a frying pan and fry the koftas for 4–5 minutes, turning to brown on all sides. At the same time add the pepper strips and cook for 3–4 minutes, to soften and brown slightly.

Open each pita bread lengthways, place a lettuce leaf in each, and add a kofta, a few strips of red pepper, and a sprig of cilantro. Serve the wraps with the minted cream.

3 tablespoons mayonnaise

few drops Tabasco sauce

1 teaspoon sun-dried tomato paste

5–6 oz. lobster meat or wild crayfish tails, freshly cooked

4 x 8-inch Flour Tortillas (see page 60)

2 handfuls mesclun with herbs

lemon wedges, to serve

guacamole

1 ripe avocado

1 tablespoon freshly squeezed lime juice

1 vine-ripened tomato, seeded and finely chopped

1 garlic clove, crushed

1 scallion, finely chopped

1 tablespoon chopped fresh cilantro

½ teaspoon ground red chile or ½ fresh hot chile, seeded and chopped

salt and freshly ground black pepper

makes 8 serves 4

For a special treat I like to make these wraps with fresh lobster, but they are equally delicious when made with wild crayfish tails. If you wish to use fresh lobsters, two 1-pound lobsters should yield sufficient meat for this recipe.

shellfish cocktail wraps
with guacamole

To make the guacamole, cut the avocado in half, remove the pit, and peel. Mash the flesh in a bowl with the lime juice, then stir in the tomato, garlic, scallion, cilantro, and chile. Season with salt and freshly ground black pepper.

Mix the mayonnaise, Tabasco, and sun-dried tomato paste together in a bowl. If using lobster, chop the meat into bite-size pieces. Add the lobster or crayfish tails to the bowl and mix together.

Lay the tortillas out on a clean work surface and top each one with guacamole, mesclun, and shellfish cocktail. Roll each wrap tightly and cut in half. Serve with lemon wedges.

Griddled zucchini slices make an ideal wrap for a stylish appetizer that is packed full of flavor. You can also try Roquefort or dolcelatte cheese as alternatives to the Gorgonzola.

zucchini rolls

2 zucchini

2 tablespoons olive oil

1 teaspoon freshly squeezed lemon juice

2½ oz. creamy Gorgonzola cheese

2½ oz. ricotta cheese

¼ cup walnuts, finely chopped

12 mint leaves

small handful of fresh chives, cut into 2-inch lengths

chile oil, for sprinkling

freshly ground black pepper

a ridged stovetop grill pan

makes 12 serves 4

Trim the ends off the zucchini and cut a thin slice, lengthways, off each side and discard. Then cut each zucchini into six slices lengthways, about ¼ inch thick. Mix the olive oil and lemon juice together. Brush over the zucchini slices and sprinkle with freshly ground black pepper.

Heat a ridged stovetop grill pan for about 4 minutes, or until hot. Put half the zucchini slices in the pan and cook until the underneath has developed brown lines from the ridges in the pan. Turn over and repeat on the other side, but do not overcook or they may split when rolled. Transfer to a plate to cool and cook the remaining zucchini slices.

Mix the Gorgonzola and ricotta cheeses together and spread over the zucchini slices. Sprinkle each with a few chopped walnuts and place a mint leaf and a few chives at one end, so they overlap the edge. Starting from this end gently roll up.

Arrange on serving plates with the mint and chives uppermost. Serve the rolls sprinkled with a little chile oil and freshly ground black pepper.

These wraps are the perfect make-ahead appetizer, especially since the tabbouleh filling will taste even better than when freshly made. Make the filling up to 24 hours in advance, cover, and leave in a cool place for the flavors to infuse. At the last minute, just fill the tortillas and serve.

smoked ham and tabbouleh cones

⅓ cup bulgur

2 tablespoons chopped fresh mint

3 tablespoons chopped fresh parsley

2 scallions, finely chopped

2 inches cucumber, halved, seeded, and diced

2 vine-ripened tomatoes, diced

1 garlic clove, crushed

3 tablespoons olive oil

1 tablespoon freshly squeezed lemon juice

4 x 9-inch Garlic and Cilantro Flour Tortillas (see page 60)

4 large thin slices smoked ham, about 6½ oz.

salt and freshly ground black pepper

makes 8 serves 4

Put the bulgur in a bowl, cover with hot water, and let soak for 30 minutes. Drain well and tip back into the bowl.

Add the mint, parsley, scallions, cucumber, tomatoes, garlic, olive oil, and lemon juice and toss together. Season with a little salt and freshly ground black pepper. Cover and leave for the flavors to infuse.

Cut the tortillas and ham slices in half and place a piece of ham on top of each tortilla. Roll up one at a time into cone shapes and fill with some tabbouleh. Secure with a toothpick or place seam-side down. Arrange in a serving dish or serve 2 per person in individual bowls.

Flautas are usually made with corn tortillas, but are equally enjoyable made using flour tortillas if you find these easier to buy or make. Whichever you choose, fill and cook in the same way; both are delicious and make the perfect appetizer to serve with drinks.

corn flautas
with tomato salsa

6½ oz. cooked chicken breast fillets

2½ oz. feta cheese, crumbled

2 tablespoons chopped fresh cilantro

4 scallions, chopped

1 small fresh red chile, seeded and finely chopped

8 x 6-inch Corn Tortillas (see page 61)

sunflower oil, for frying

sour cream, to serve

tomato salsa

6½ oz. cherry tomatoes, roughly chopped

½ onion, finely chopped

1 tablespoon chopped fresh cilantro

grated zest and freshly squeezed juice of ½ lime

1 tablespoon olive oil

1 mild fresh chile e.g. jalapeño, chopped (optional)

makes 16 serves 4–6

To make the salsa, put the cherry tomatoes, onion, and cilantro in a bowl. Add the grated lime zest and juice, olive oil, and chile, if using, and gently mix together. Cover and set aside to allow the flavors to mingle.

Cut the chicken into thin strips. In a bowl, mix together the chicken, feta cheese, cilantro, scallions, and chile. Wrap the tortillas in foil and warm in the oven, to soften, or wrap in microwave plastic wrap and heat for about 30–45 seconds in a microwave oven.

Place a spoonful of chicken filling on one edge of each tortilla and roll up into flutes, tucking the ends in. Secure with a toothpick. Cover with plastic wrap until ready to cook, to prevent them from drying out.

Heat a heavy-based nonstick frying pan filled with oil to a depth of about 1 inch, until the oil is hot. Add half the flautas and fry for about 3 minutes, until crisp and golden, turning frequently. Drain on paper towels and keep hot while cooking the remaining flautas.

Remove the toothpicks, cut each flauta in half diagonally, and serve with the tomato salsa and sour cream.

4 oz. crab meat

2 oz. cooked and shelled shrimp, chopped

4 canned water chestnuts, finely chopped

2 scallions, finely chopped

1 inch fresh ginger, peeled and grated

1 small fresh chile, seeded and finely chopped

1 tablespoon chopped fresh cilantro

1 tablespoon light soy sauce

20 x 3½-inch round wonton wrappers

toasted sesame seeds, to sprinkle

a steamer

soy and ginger dipping sauce

3 tablespoons light soy sauce

3 tablespoons Chinese rice wine or dry sherry

½ inch fresh ginger, peeled and sliced

makes 20 serves 4–6

These bite-size morsels are typical of Chinese dim sum—they look elegant, smell tantalizing, and taste good! Use fresh crab meat for the very best flavor. If you do need to use frozen crab meat, make sure it is well drained before using.

crab wonton wraps with dipping sauce

In a bowl mix together the crab meat, shrimp, water chestnuts, scallions, ginger, chile, cilantro, and soy sauce.

Brush the edges of a wonton wrapper with water. Place a heaped teaspoon of filling in the center. Draw up the edges and press together. Repeat to make 20 wonton wraps. Cover until ready to cook.

In a small bowl, combine the dipping sauce ingredients.

Put a layer of parchment paper in the base of a steamer and arrange the wonton wraps in the steamer, making sure they do not touch each other. Place over a pan of boiling water, cover and steam for 5 minutes. Cook in batches if necessary.

Sprinkle with toasted sesame seeds and serve with the soy and ginger dipping sauce.

simple meals

This recipe serves 4 but easily lends itself to making for just 1 or 2 for a midday meal, just reduce the quantities to suit. Any remaining avocado will keep for up to 24 hours, if left attached to the skin and pit. Brush a little lemon juice over the cut surface to help prevent discoloration.

6 slices thick-cut bacon

2 teaspoons whole-grain mustard

¼ cup extra virgin olive oil

1 tablespoon freshly squeezed lemon juice

2 handfuls baby spinach leaves

1 ripe avocado, pitted, peeled, and sliced

4 x 9-inch Mediterranean Herb Flour Tortillas (see page 60)

5 oz. ripe Brie, sliced

salt and freshly ground black pepper

cranberry-and-onion chutney or cranberry sauce, to serve

makes 4 serves 4

avocado, brie, and bacon wraps

Preheat the broiler to medium.

Put the bacon on the broiler pan and broil for 3–4 minutes per side or until cooked and the fat is golden and crisp. Drain on paper towels and cut into pieces with scissors.

Put the mustard, olive oil, and lemon juice in a small bowl. Add salt and pepper to season and whisk to make a dressing.

Put the spinach in a bowl, add the bacon and avocado, then pour over the dressing and toss lightly to coat. Divide the salad between the wraps and top with Brie slices. Fold one end of each tortilla to enclose the filling, then roll up and serve immediately with chutney or cranberry sauce.

Corn tortillas, pinto beans, and chiles are synonymous with Mexican cooking. This recipe combines chicken with a fiery tomato sauce as a filling for the soft tortillas, which are topped with sour cream and cheddar cheese before baking. It makes a perfect lunch or supper dish served with a crisp lettuce salad.

chile chicken enchiladas

3 tablespoons sunflower oil

16 oz. skinless chicken breast fillets, cut into strips

1 large onion, chopped

1 fresh red chile, seeded and finely chopped

1 garlic clove, crushed

2 tablespoons tomato paste

14-oz. can chopped tomatoes

14-oz. can pinto beans, rinsed and drained

1 tablespoon chopped fresh cilantro

8 x 8-inch Corn Tortillas, warmed (see page 61)

⅔ cup sour cream

2½ oz. sharp cheddar cheese, grated

salt and freshly ground black pepper

shredded scallions, to sprinkle

serves 4–6

Preheat the oven to 375°F.

Heat 2 tablespoons of the oil in a large nonstick frying pan, add the chicken and stir-fry for 4–5 minutes, or until golden. Remove with a slotted spoon, put into a bowl, and set aside.

Add the remaining oil to the pan, then the onion, and fry for 5 minutes. Add the chile and garlic and fry for 1–2 minutes more, or until the onions are soft and golden. Stir in the tomato paste, canned tomatoes, and ⅓ cup cold water. Cook for 2–3 minutes and season with salt and freshly ground black pepper.

Add just under half the sauce to the chicken with the beans and cilantro and mix together. Spoon 2 heaped tablespoons of the chicken mixture onto the middle of each warmed tortilla and roll up to enclose the filling. Place seam-side down in a greased baking dish and top with the remaining tomato sauce.

Spoon the sour cream along the center of the tortillas and sprinkle with the grated cheese. Bake in the preheated oven for 15–20 minutes or until golden and bubbling. Sprinkle over the scallions and serve.

This mustard and honey-glazed steak makes a succulent and tasty filling for the salsa-flavored wraps. To make them less messy to eat, serve them "fajita style", made by enclosing the filling at one end, to form a pocket. Serve one per person for lunch or allow two for a more substantial supper dish along with an extra bowl of salad.

mustard and honey-glazed steak fajitas

2 tablespoons extra virgin olive oil

2 tablespoons honey

1 tablespoon balsamic vinegar

2 tablespoons Dijon mustard

2 x 6-oz. sirloin or rump steaks

3 tablespoons mayonnaise

4 x 10-inch Salsa Flour Tortillas (see page 60)

2 handfuls bitter lettuce

4 scallions, thinly sliced

8 small vine-ripened tomatoes, quartered

freshly ground black pepper

a ridged stovetop grill pan (optional)

makes 4 serves 2–4

Preheat the oven to 350°F. In a shallow dish, mix together the olive oil, honey, balsamic vinegar, and 1 tablespoon of the mustard with a generous sprinkling of freshly ground black pepper. Trim the steaks of any fat, then add to the marinade, turning them over to coat both sides. Cover and leave in a cool place to marinate for 30 minutes, or longer if time allows. Mix the remaining mustard and the mayonnaise together.

Wrap the tortillas in foil and warm them in the oven for 10 minutes. (You can also warm the tortilla wraps in a microwave oven for about 45–60 seconds. If you do, cook the steaks first.)

Heat a heavy-based frying pan or ridged stovetop grill pan until hot, then cook the steaks for 1½–2 minutes each side, or longer if you prefer your steak well done. Slice the steaks.

Divide the lettuce, scallions, and tomatoes between the tortillas and top with the steak slices. Fold in the sides of the wrap to overlap and then tuck one end underneath to enclose the bottom of the filling. Serve topped with a spoonful of mustard mayonnaise or serve it separately.

These Moroccan-inspired wraps are perfect for an informal lunch. Serve the kebabs, a dish of couscous, and a pile of chapatti wraps and invite your guests to help themselves.

lamb and couscous salad wraps with harissa dressing

3 tablespoons olive oil
1 teaspoon freshly squeezed lemon juice
1 teaspoon ground coriander
½ teaspoon ground turmeric
1 teaspoon harissa paste
1¼ pounds lean lamb from the leg
2 small red onions, each cut into 8 wedges
1 cup couscous
¾ cup boiling vegetable broth
8 x 6½-inch Chapattis (see page 62)
4 scallions, shredded
8 dried apricots, chopped
2 miniature preserved lemons, thinly sliced (optional)
3 tablespoons toasted flaked almonds
1 tablespoon chopped fresh cilantro
8 wooden skewers, soaked in water

harissa dressing
⅔ cup plain yogurt
2 teaspoons harissa paste
1 tablespoon chopped fresh cilantro
salt and freshly ground black pepper

makes 8 serves 4

In a shallow dish mix 2 tablespoons of the olive oil, the lemon juice, coriander, turmeric, and harissa paste together. Cut the lamb into chunks, add to the dish, toss to coat, cover, and let marinate in a cool place for 30 minutes or longer, if time allows. Next make the harissa dressing: in a small bowl, mix together the yogurt, harissa paste, and cilantro and season with salt and freshly ground black pepper.

Preheat the broiler to medium. Thread the chunks of lamb onto the skewers with the onion wedges. Place on a broiler rack and brush with the remaining marinade. Put the couscous in a saucepan, pour over the hot broth, cover, and let stand for 10 minutes, stirring occasionally.

Put the kebabs under the preheated broiler and cook for 8–10 minutes, until browned on the outside but pink in the center.

Warm the chapattis in a microwave oven for 1–1½ minutes, or in a warm oven, wrapped in foil. Heat the couscous for 1–2 minutes to warm through, if necessary. Stir in the remaining olive oil, the scallions, apricots, lemons (if using), almonds, and cilantro.

Either serve the warm chapattis with the kebabs, couscous, and dressing separately, or assemble first by topping each chapatti with a little couscous, then the meat and onions from a kebab. Drizzle the dressing over, before rolling up and securing with a toothpick if wished.

Quails' eggs are the perfect size for these summery salad wraps but you can always substitute two hard-boiled hens' eggs cut into wedges if preferred.

salade Niçoise crêpe wraps

2 x 4 oz. fresh tuna fillets

1 tablespoon olive oil

8 quails' eggs

12 baby new potatoes, halved

3½ oz. thin green beans, halved

6 baby plum tomatoes on the vine, halved

8 pitted black olives, halved

4 anchovy fillets, cut into thin strips

½ small red onion, thinly sliced

5 tablespoons basil oil

1 tablespoon freshly squeezed lemon juice

8 Crêpes (see page 63)

2 tablespoons freshly grated Parmesan cheese

salt and freshly ground black pepper

makes 8 serves 4

Heat a broiler pan until hot. Brush the tuna with olive oil and season with freshly ground black pepper. Cook the tuna for 2–3 minutes per side and then set aside to cool. Cook the eggs in boiling water for 3 minutes, or until hard-boiled. Plunge into cold water, shell, and cut in half.

Cook the potatoes in boiling, lightly salted water for 6 minutes, add the beans, and cook for 4 minutes, or until both are tender. Drain and refresh in cold water and drain well.

In a bowl, toss together the potatoes, beans, tomatoes, olives, anchovies, and onion. Whisk 3 tablespoons of the basil oil with the lemon juice and pour over the salad ingredients. Cut the tuna into thick strips and add these and the eggs to the salad. Gently toss together.

Fold the crêpes into four and fill with the salade Niçoise mixture. Arrange on 4 serving plates, drizzle over the remaining basil oil, sprinkle with the Parmesan cheese, and serve.

Fennel, peppers, and sage, with their distinctive Mediterranean flavors, topped with melted strings of mozzarella provide the succulent filling for these zucchini crêpe rolls. You could also use Taleggio or Fontina cheese, both of which will ooze deliciously out of the crêpes as you cut into them.

Mediterranean vegetable crêpe rolls

1 red bell pepper, seeded and cut into thick strips

1 orange bell pepper, seeded and cut into thick strips

2 onions, cut into wedges

1 fennel bulb, cut into wedges

3 tablespoons olive or sunflower oil

1 garlic clove, crushed

8 Zucchini Crêpes (see page 63)

2 teaspoons chopped fresh sage

2½ oz. mozzarella cheese, sliced

1 cup grated cheddar or Parmesan cheese

3 tablespoons fresh breadcrumbs

salt and freshly ground black pepper

makes 8 serves 4

Preheat the oven to 375°F.

Toss the peppers, onions, and fennel together with the oil and garlic and set aside. Make the zucchini crêpes and keep them warm by wrapping them in a clean kitchen towel while you make the filling.

Heat a large griddle pan until hot and cook the vegetables over medium heat for about 8–10 minutes, or until they are just tender and beginning to char slightly. Stir in the sage and season with salt and freshly ground black pepper.

Divide the vegetables between the crêpes, top with the mozzarella, and roll up to enclose the filling. Arrange in a shallow ovenproof dish and sprinkle over the cheddar or Parmesan cheese and breadcrumbs.

Bake for 15–20 minutes, or until the cheese has melted. If preferred, finish under a preheated broiler for about 5 minutes.

These pancake rolls convey the essence of the renowned Peking duck, but with the preparation cut to the minimum. To simplify serving, and make for a very sociable meal, just serve dishes of duck strips, cucumber, scallions, and sauce with the warm pancakes and each person can make their own.

Chinese pancake rolls with duck

3 x 6½-oz. duck breasts

1 tablespoon honey

1 teaspoon soy sauce

12–16 Chinese pancakes for Peking duck (you can buy these at your local Chinese restaurant or market)

½ cup hoisin or plum sauce

10 scallions, cut in half widthways, then sliced lengthways

½ cucumber, cut into matchsticks about 4 inches long

salt

½ cup sweet chile sauce, to serve (optional)

a bamboo steamer (optional)

makes 12–16 serves 4

Preheat the oven to 400°F.

Rub the skin-side of the duck breasts with salt. Leave uncovered in the fridge for at least 2 and up to 8 hours, if time allows, to draw out the moisture. Wipe dry and prick all over with a fork.

Heat a frying pan until hot and cook the duck breasts skin-side down for 5 minutes, drawing off the fat as it is released. Transfer to a rack in a roasting pan, placing the skin side uppermost, and roast for 10 minutes. Meanwhile mix the honey and soy sauce together.

Brush the honey mixture over the duck and cook for 5–10 minutes more, depending how well cooked you like duck. Let rest for 5 minutes, then cut into strips. Warm the Chinese pancakes in a bamboo steamer over simmering water or stack on a plate, cover with foil, and place the plate over a pan of simmering water.

To serve, spread a little hoisin sauce on each pancake, fill with a few duck strips, scallion strips, and cucumber matchsticks, and roll up. Serve immediately with sweet chile sauce, if wished.

Serve these translucent Asian-style wraps with a vegetable stir-fry. Just stir-fry a combination of baby bok choi, cut in half lengthways, sugar snap peas, and shiitake mushrooms with a little crushed garlic while you are cooking the wraps.

salmon in rice-paper wrappers

4 x 3½-oz. salmon fillets

grated zest and freshly squeezed juice of 1 lime

2 inches fresh ginger, peeled and grated

2 tablespoons chopped fresh cilantro

4 scallions, chopped

1 garlic clove, crushed

8 x 8-inch Vietnamese rice-paper wrappers

¼ cup sunflower oil

¼ cup Thai fish sauce or oyster sauce

1 tablespoon toasted sesame seeds

makes 8 serves 4

Cut each piece of salmon in half. Mix the lime juice and zest, ginger, cilantro, scallions, and garlic together in a bowl. Spread over the tops of the salmon pieces.

Fill a shallow dish large enough to hold the rice-paper wrappers with warm water. Soak them for 15–20 seconds or until just soft and pliable. Place on a damp kitchen towel and blot to remove excess water. Place a piece of fish on each round. Fold in the sides of the wrappers and roll to enclose the fish.

Heat the oil in a frying pan over medium heat. Add the fish parcels and fry for 2–3 minutes per side, or until the rice paper is golden and the fish is just tender. Drain on kitchen towels.

Arrange two rice-paper wrappers on each serving plate, drizzle over a little Thai fish sauce, and sprinkle with sesame seeds. Serve with stir-fried vegetables, if wished.

food on the go

Outdoor feasts are always occasions to enjoy. The combination of wafer-thin slices of prosciutto, pecorino cheese, juicy ripe peaches, and fresh arugula leaves makes a perfect blend of flavors for a summer eating experience worth savoring.

2 tablespoons pesto sauce

4 oz. farmer's cheese

4 x 10-inch Flour Tortillas (see page 60)

4 oz. prosciutto, very thinly sliced

2 ripe peaches, peeled, stoned, and sliced

2 handfuls arugula leaves

1 oz. pecorino cheese shavings

few fresh basil leaves, to sprinkle

balsamic vinegar and olive oil, to drizzle

freshly ground black pepper

makes 8 serves 4

prosciutto, peach, and pecorino cornets

In a small bowl, mix the pesto sauce and farmer's cheese together. Spread over the tortillas and then cut each in half.

Tear the prosciutto into smaller pieces. Divide the peach slices, arugula, and prosciutto between the tortillas and sprinkle with black pepper. Roll each one into a cone shape and secure with a toothpick if wished.

Arrange on serving plates and sprinkle over the pecorino cheese shavings and basil leaves. Drizzle with balsamic vinegar and olive oil and serve immediately. If transporting to a picnic, pack in a cooler and take the olive oil and balsamic vinegar separately to drizzle over just before eating.

Crêpes make wonderful wrappers for savory fillings and are a great alternative to tortillas. This recipe fuses Western-style crêpes flavored with scallions with an Asian crispy vegetable, ginger-marinated pork, and hoisin sauce filling.

Asian pork crêpe wraps

2 tablespoons sunflower oil

2 tablespoons soy sauce

2 inches fresh ginger, peeled and grated

2 teaspoons ground coriander

14 oz. pork tenderloin, sliced

8 Scallion Crêpes (see page 63)

1 cup sliced Chinese cabbage

1 cup bean sprouts

3 scallions, cut into fine strips

6 tablespoons hoisin sauce

makes 8 serves 4

In a shallow dish, mix together the oil, soy sauce, ginger, and ground coriander. Add the pork slices and toss to coat.

Heat a nonstick frying pan or wok and stir-fry the pork for 3–4 minutes, until cooked. Remove and set aside to cool.

To assemble, fill each crêpe with some Chinese greens, bean sprouts, and scallions. Top with a few pork slices and some hoisin sauce. Roll up to enclose the filling and tuck one end under, fajita style.

If you are making these for a picnic, spread the hoisin sauce over each crêpe first and then top with the remaining filling ingredients and roll as above.

Eggplant slices make the perfect wrap for easy-to-prepare alfresco eating. Packed with the flavors of the Mediterranean—feta cheese, basil, sun-dried tomatoes, and pine nuts—what could be better for an outing on a summer's day?

eggplant rolls

1 large eggplant

2 tablespoons olive oil

½ small red onion

¼ cup fresh basil leaves

4 oz. feta cheese, crumbled

4 half-dried tomatoes in oil, drained and chopped

⅓ cup pine nuts, toasted

freshly ground black pepper

a ridged stovetop grill pan

makes 8 serves 4

Trim the stalk off the eggplant and cut lengthways into eight thin slices, about ¼ inch thick. Heat a ridged stovetop grill pan until it is really hot. Brush both sides of the eggplant slices with oil and cook, in batches, for 1½–2 minutes on each side, until tender and soft enough to roll up. Set aside to cool.

Cut the onion into thin slivers, lengthways. Reserve a few small leaves of basil and shred the remainder. In a bowl gently toss the feta cheese, tomatoes, shredded basil, and all but 1 tablespoon of the pine nuts together and season with freshly ground black pepper.

Pile a spoonful of the feta mix on the end third of each eggplant slice and add a few slivers of onion. Roll up and place seam-side down on a serving plate or pack in a picnic container. Serve sprinkled with the remaining pine nuts and reserved basil leaves.

I like the contrast of the tart peppery note of the watercress with the sweet juicy mango and spice-laced basmati rice in these chapatti wraps. If you prefer, you could replace the watercress with a mixed-leaf salad such as mesclun or baby mustard greens.

fragrant rice with mango and turkey wraps

generous pinch of saffron

1¼ cups hot chicken broth

3 tablespoons sunflower oil

6 oz. raw turkey breast, cut into strips

2 shallots, chopped

½ cup basmati rice

3 cardamom pods, crushed, black seeds retained and the pods discarded

2 cloves

½ stick cinnamon

¼ cup mayonnaise

2 teaspoons curry paste

4 x 8-inch Chapattis (see page 62)

2 tablespoons cashew nuts, toasted

1 ripe mango, peeled, stoned, and cut into small slices

2 handfuls watercress

freshly ground black pepper

makes 8 serves 4

Stir the saffron into the hot broth and set aside. Heat 2 tablespoons of the oil in a frying pan, add the turkey strips and shallots, and sauté for 3–4 minutes to brown slightly.

Meanwhile, heat the remaining oil in a nonstick saucepan, add the rice, and cook, stirring, for 1 minute. Add the cardamom seeds, cloves, and cinnamon and cook for 1 minute more.

Pour in the saffron stock and bring to a boil. Add the turkey and shallots, season with black pepper, cover, and cook gently for about 12 minutes, or until the rice is tender and all the liquid has been absorbed. Remove the cloves and cinnamon stick, discard, and set the rice aside to cool.

Mix the mayonnaise and curry paste together and spread over the chapattis. Stir the cashew nuts into the rice and then put a quarter of the rice mix on each chapatti and top with mango slices and watercress. Roll up firmly to enclose the filling and cut in half to serve. If the wraps are to go, wrap in plastic wrap and pack in a cooler.

Tortillas, which originated from Latin America, are perfect for picnics and packed lunches as an alternative to a sandwich. These flat breads can be wrapped around almost any filling; here I have wrapped crisp vegetables inside a tortilla spread with garlicky hummus.

lemon and garlic hummus tortilla rolls

14-oz. can chickpeas, rinsed and drained

grated zest and freshly squeezed juice of 1 lemon

2 garlic cloves, chopped

2 tablespoons extra virgin olive oil

1 tablespoon tahini paste

4 x 10-inch Flour Tortillas (see page 60)

2 carrots, cut into thin sticks

2 celery ribs, chopped

4 sun-dried tomatoes in oil, drained and sliced

½ small onion, thinly sliced

1 cup mache

salt and freshly ground black pepper

makes 8 serves 4

To make the hummus, put the drained chickpeas in a food processor with the lemon juice, garlic, and olive oil. Blend until semi-smooth before adding the tahini. Season with salt and pepper and blend until smooth. Finally, stir in the grated lemon zest.

Lay the tortillas on a clean work surface and spread a quarter of the hummus over each. Divide the carrots, celery, sun-dried tomatoes, onion, and mache between the tortillas, scattering over the center in a band. Season and tightly roll up each wrap.

Cut each wrap in half and serve or wrap in baking parchment and pack in a cooler.

These wraps are best made as close to eating as possible, ideally within an hour as the nori will soften once filled. For a hands-on picnic, take separate containers of the individual ingredients, plus the cooked rice and nori sheets, and let everyone make their own wraps, choosing their favorite fillings.

sushi wraps

1 cup Japanese short-grain rice

2 tablespoons rice vinegar

1 tablespoon mirin

½ teaspoon sugar

½ teaspoon salt

½ small avocado

1 tablespoon freshly squeezed lemon juice

4 sheets nori, each cut into four

2 tablespoons wasabi paste

3½ oz. fresh tuna fillet, cut into 8 fingers

½ yellow bell pepper, seeded and cut into sticks

50 g smoked salmon slices, cut into 8 pieces

8 cooked and shelled tiger shrimp

1½ inches cucumber, cut into sticks

pickled ginger and shoyu sauce, to serve

makes 16 serves 4

Put the rice in a nonstick saucepan with 1½ cups cold water, bring to a boil, cover tightly, and cook over a very low heat for 12 minutes. Remove from the heat and let stand for 15 minutes. Mix the rice vinegar, mirin, sugar, and salt together and fold into the rice. Cover and let cool.

Cut the avocado into slices. Put the lemon juice in a shallow dish, add the avocado, and toss to coat.

Spread 2 tablespoons of rice over a piece of nori. Add a small amount of wasabi paste and top with a piece each of tuna, pepper, and avocado. You may find this easier if you hold the nori on the palm of your hand to fill. Roll up into a cone shape. Dampen the final edge with water or shoyu sauce to stick together. Fill 7 more squares of nori in the same way.

Fill the remaining nori squares with rice topped with a smoked salmon piece, a shrimp, and a couple of cucumber sticks. Serve the sushi wraps with small dishes of ginger and shoyu sauce.

I have included the recipe for Caesar dressing, which is certainly worth the effort for the very best flavor and really only takes a few minutes to make. If, however, you are short on time for a spur-of-the-moment picnic, make sure you use the best quality prepared Caesar dressing you can find.

2½ oz. Parmesan cheese

4 x 10-inch Flour Tortillas (see page 60)

8–12 romaine heart lettuce leaves, depending on size

10 oz. cooked skinless chicken fillets, sliced

Caesar dressing

2 garlic cloves, chopped

2 anchovy fillets in oil, drained and chopped

1 egg yolk

1 tablespoon white wine vinegar

1 tablespoon Dijon mustard

3 tablespoons light olive oil

3 tablespoons sunflower oil

freshly ground black pepper

makes 8 serves 4

chicken Caesar salad
wraps with Caesar dressing

To prepare the Caesar dressing, mash the garlic and anchovies to a paste in a small bowl. Put in a food processor with the egg yolk, vinegar, mustard, and a little black pepper. Blend together briefly, then, with the motor still running, add the oils in a slow trickle through the feed tube, as if you were making mayonnaise.

Use a potato peeler to make Parmesan cheese shavings. Lay the tortillas out on a clean work surface and top each one with 2–3 lettuce leaves, a few chicken breast slices, and some Parmesan shavings. Drizzle with Caesar dressing.

Roll each wrap tightly and cut in half diagonally. Wrap in waxed paper and pack in a cooler or serve as required.

The flavor of the toasted sesame seeds in the crêpes complements the ginger and chile flavored shrimp, but they are equally delicious wrapped in scallion-flavored or whole-wheat crêpes.

sesame crêpe wraps and piquant shrimp with aioli

32 large uncooked tiger shrimp, shelled and deveined, tails on

1 lemongrass stalk, chopped

2 inches fresh ginger, peeled and chopped

1 fresh red chile, seeded

¼ cup olive oil

1 tablespoon freshly squeezed lemon juice

8 Sesame Crêpes (see page 63)

1 small head curly endive

small bunch fresh flat leaf parsley

garlic and lemon aioli

1 garlic clove, chopped

½ teaspoon salt

grated zest and freshly squeezed juice of ½ lemon

1 egg yolk

¼ cup extra virgin olive oil

¼ cup sunflower oil

freshly ground black pepper

makes 8 serves 4

Remove the tails from 24 of the shrimp and put all the shrimp in a shallow dish. Place the lemongrass, ginger, chile, olive oil, and lemon juice in a food processor and blend to a rough paste. Add to the shrimp, toss together, cover, and marinate in the refrigerator for 30 minutes, or longer if time allows.

To make the aioli, place the garlic, salt, lemon juice, and egg yolk in the cleaned food processor and pulse briefly to combine. With the motor running, slowly trickle in the two oils through the feeder tube until the aioli is thick and emulsified. Season with freshly ground black pepper and stir in the lemon zest.

Heat a frying pan until hot, add the shrimp and marinade and stir-fry for 2–3 minutes, until the shrimp turn pink, but don't overcook or they will become tough. Set aside to cool.

To assemble, fill each sesame crêpe with some endive leaves and top with the shrimp, making sure a shrimp with its tail is at the top. Scatter over a few sprigs of parsley and roll tightly to enclose the filling. Fold the bottom end under to secure. Serve with the garlic and lemon aioli.

basic recipes

Flour tortillas are readily available, but if you make them, you can add your favorite herbs and spices. They are more pliable than corn tortillas, but it is worth warming them slightly (even for a cold filling) to assist in the rolling and folding and prevent cracking.

flour tortillas

2 cups all-purpose flour
½ teaspoon salt
¼ cup shortening or lard
⅔ cup lukewarm water

makes 9–10 x 8-inch, 8 x 9-inch, or 6 x 10-inch

Variations

Garlic and Cilantro
Add 2 crushed garlic cloves and 1 tablespoon finely chopped fresh cilantro.

Mediterranean Herb
Add 1 tablespoon each finely chopped fresh oregano and flat leaf parsley.

Salsa
Mix 4 teaspoons tomato paste with half the water, and add enough of the remaining water to mix to a dough. Add 1 teaspoon ground red chile, 1 crushed garlic clove, 2 teaspoons finely chopped fresh flat leaf parsley, and 1 tablespoon finely chopped fresh oregano.

Mix the flour and salt together in a large bowl. Rub in the shortening or lard using your fingertips. Stir in enough water to mix to a smooth dough. Knead for 3–4 minutes, then place in a clean bowl, cover, and leave to rest for 15 minutes. If adding any flavorings, knead into the dough before setting aside.

Divide into individual pieces depending on the size you wish to make. On a lightly floured surface roll out each piece of dough, very thinly, into rounds of your selected size. Keep the dough balls and rolled tortillas covered so they stay moist.

Heat a large heavy-based griddle or frying pan until hot and cook the tortillas, one at a time, for 1½–2 minutes, turning over as soon as the surface starts to bubble. Take care not to overcook; they should stay soft and flexible, otherwise they will break when rolled. Wrap the cooked tortillas in a clean kitchen towel to keep them soft and warm, while you cook the rest.

To re-warm tortillas, place on a microwave-proof plate, wrap with microwave plastic wrap and microwave for about 10 seconds for one, or 30 seconds for four. To warm in the oven, wrap in aluminum foil and place in a preheated oven at 350°F for 10 minutes.

Corn tortillas use masa harina. Distinctive in flavor, it makes a more dense tortilla than the flour version. For a lighter, easier-to-roll tortilla, replace up to half the masa harina with all-purpose flour. It is not the same as cornmeal, which cannot be substituted successfully.

corn tortillas

2 cups masa harina

½ teaspoon salt

1 cup water

1 tablespoon corn oil

**makes 12 x 6-inch
or 8 x 8-inch**

Place the masa harina, salt, water, and oil in a bowl and mix together to a dough. Turn onto a lightly floured surface and knead well for 3–4 minutes, until firm and smooth. Put in a clean bowl, cover, and leave to rest for 30 minutes.

Divide the dough into 12 or 8, depending on the size of tortilla you wish to make. Keep covered. Put a ball of dough between two sheets of plastic wrap. Flatten gently with the palm of your hand, then roll out into a 6- or 8-inch diameter round tortilla, turning a quarter turn with each roll. You can use a tortilla press or chapatti press instead of a rolling pin.

Heat an ungreased griddle or heavy-based frying pan over moderate heat. Peel off the top layer of plastic wrap. Turn the tortilla onto your hand, remove the remaining plastic wrap, and transfer to the pan. Cook for 45 seconds, or until the underside is blistered and golden speckles are just beginning to appear. Using a spatula, turn over and cook for another 30 seconds.

If using immediately, wrap the cooked tortillas in a clean kitchen towel or wrap in foil and place in a preheated oven at 300°F to keep warm while cooking the remainder.

To reheat, either place on a microwave-proof plate, cover with microwave plastic wrap and cook on full power for 40–50 seconds or sprinkle with a little cold water, wrap in foil, and place in a preheated oven at 350°F for 10 minutes.

These Indian flat breads are traditionally made with a very fine whole-wheat flour called atta, sometimes simply labelled chapatti flour. Blended atta flours contain both whole-wheat and white flour and give a slightly lighter chapatti. The blended flours are perfect for wraps, as they make the wraps easier to roll.

chapattis

1¾ cups atta or chapatti flour

½ teaspoon salt

about ⅔ cup water

1 teaspoon vegetable oil

**makes 8 x 6½-inch
or 5 x 8-inch**

Put the flour and salt into a bowl. Add the water slowly, adding just enough to mix to a soft dough. Knead in the oil.

Turn onto a lightly floured surface and knead for 5–6 minutes, until smooth. Place in a lightly oiled bowl, cover with a damp kitchen towel and let rest for 30 minutes. On a lightly floured surface, divide the dough into 8, or 5 if making large chapattis, and shape into balls.

Flatten the dough using the palm of your hand, then roll out into a 6½- or 8-inch round. Stack on top of each other with sheets of plastic wrap in between to keep the chapattis moist.

Heat a cast-iron griddle or heavy-based frying pan over medium heat until hot. Brush any excess flour from the chapattis and place on the griddle or in the pan. Cook for 45 seconds, or until the top side begins to bubble and white specks appear on the underside. Turn over and cook for a further 30–45 seconds. Remove, place on a plate and cover with a clean kitchen towel to keep moist.

They are best served fresh. To reheat, wrap in foil and place in a preheated oven at 350°F for 10 minutes, or sprinkle with a few drops of water, wrap in microwave-proof plastic wrap and reheat for a few seconds in the microwave. Allow around 10–15 seconds for one and 40–50 seconds for the whole quantity.

Make a batch of crêpes up to 24 hours in advance so they can be filled and served in minutes. Most recipes in this book use cold crêpes, but if you need to reheat them, wrap the stack of crêpes in foil and place in a preheated oven at 350°F for 10 minutes to warm through.

crêpes

1 cup all-purpose flour

pinch of salt

1 egg

about 1¼ cups milk

sunflower oil for frying

makes 8

Variations

Sesame Crêpes
Add 1 tablespoon lightly toasted sesame seeds to the finished batter.

Buckwheat Pancakes
Use ½ cup buckwheat flour and 3 tablespoons all-purpose flour in place of the 1 cup all-purpose flour. Reduce the milk to ⅔ cup.

Scallion Crêpes
Stir 2 finely chopped scallions into the finished batter.

Zucchini Crêpes
Stir ¾ cup grated zucchini and 2 teaspoons chopped fresh thyme into the batter.

Whole-wheat Crêpes
Replace half the all-purpose flour with whole-wheat flour.

Sift the flour and salt into a bowl and make a well in the center. Add the egg and a little of the milk and whisk together, gradually incorporating the flour. Add the remaining milk and mix to a smooth batter. It should have the consistency of thin cream. Pour into a pitcher and set aside for 30 minutes. If the batter has thickened, add a little extra milk.

Heat a little oil in a 7- to 8-inch crêpe pan or heavy-based frying pan, or a 6-inch pan if making buckwheat pancakes, until hot. Pour off the excess oil. Add a little batter to the pan, about 3 tablespoons, tilting the pan so the batter is evenly and thinly spread over the bottom of the pan.

Cook over moderate heat for about 1 minute, or until the underside is golden and the top is set. Flip the crêpe over using a narrow spatula and cook for a further 30–45 seconds, or until it is golden. Turn onto a sheet of parchment paper and continue until all the batter is used. Stack the pancakes between layers of parchment paper. To keep them warm, cover loosely in foil and place on a baking sheet in the oven at 325°F.

index

conversion chart

Weights and measures have been rounded up
or down slightly to make measuring easier.

Measuring butter:
A US stick of butter weighs 4 oz. which is
approximately 115 g or 8 tablespoons.

Volume equivalents:

American	Metric	Imperial
1 teaspoon	5 ml	
1 tablespoon	15 ml	
¼ cup	60 ml	2 fl.oz.
⅓ cup	75 ml	2½ fl.oz.
½ cup	125 ml	4 fl.oz.
⅔ cup	150 ml	5 fl.oz. (¼ pint)
¾ cup	175 ml	6 fl.oz.
1 cup	250 ml	8 fl.oz.

Weight equivalents:

Imperial	Metric
1 oz.	30 g
2 oz.	55 g
3 oz.	85 g
3½ oz.	100 g
4 oz.	115 g
5 oz.	140 g
6 oz.	175 g
8 oz. (½ lb.)	225 g
9 oz.	250 g
10 oz.	280 g
11½ oz.	325 g
12 oz.	350 g
13 oz.	375 g
14 oz.	400 g
15 oz.	425 g
16 oz. (1 lb.)	450 g

Measurements:

Inches	Cm
¼ inch	5 mm
½ inch	1 cm
¾ inch	1.5 cm
1 inch	2.5 cm
2 inches	5 cm
3 inches	7 cm
4 inches	10 cm
5 inches	12 cm
6 inches	15 cm
7 inches	18 cm
8 inches	20 cm
9 inches	23 cm
10 inches	25 cm
11 inches	28 cm
12 inches	30 cm

Oven temperatures:

150°C	300°F	Gas 2
170°C	325°F	Gas 3
180°C	350°F	Gas 4
190°C	375°F	Gas 5
200°C	400°F	Gas 6